INTRO TO

MARKETING

ABDUL B. SUBHANI

Abbott Press books may be ordered through booksellers or by contacting:

Abbott Press
1663 Liberty Drive
Bloomington, IN 47403
www.abbottpress.com
Phone: 1-866-697-5310

Because of the dynamic nature of the Internet, any web addresses or
links contained in this book may have changed since publication and
may no longer be valid. The views expressed in this work are solely those
of the author and do not necessarily reflect the views of the publisher,
and the publisher hereby disclaims any responsibility for them.

Any people depicted in stock imagery provided by Thinkstock are
models, and such images are being used for illustrative purposes only.
Certain stock imagery © Thinkstock.

ISBN: 978-1-4582-1785-1 (sc)
ISBN: 978-1-4582-1787-5 (hc)
ISBN: 978-1-4582-1786-8 (e)

Library of Congress Control Number: 2014917038

Printed in the United States of America.

Abbott Press rev. date: 10/17/2014

To My Grandparents

Sheikh Akhtar Subhani

(1915–2002)

Sepahar Khatoon

(1923–2006)

CONTENTS

Pay-Per-Click

Social Network/ Media Marketing

Measuring Results

INTRODUCTION TO INTERNET MARKETING

Internet marketing gives business owners a marketing opportunity with immense reach and scope. Once you learn the basic principles underlying this affordable marketing strategy, you can use Internet marketing to significantly boost the Return on Investment (ROI) for your business. Being a small fish in the big sea of Internet marketers could pose a challenge when you set off to market your business online. However, being creative, consistent, and knowledgeable about the tactics involved in Internet marketing can help you to stay ahead of your competition and increase your online visibility among the relevant audience.

Benefits of Internet Marketing:

- Internet marketing is cost-effective, allowing small and medium businesses to promote their business dynamically, at a nominal cost.

- With the global reach of the web, promoting your business online gives you immense exposure, which is impossible to achieve through any other advertising media.
- It is easy to manage your Internet marketing campaign and make changes to your strategies with the multiple online tools available for different campaigns.
- With an Internet marketing strategy in place, your business is open 24/7, and you do not ever have to worry about a customer not being able to reach you.
- If you have made an investment in creating a website for your business, Internet marketing can help generate returns.
- Internet marketing broadens the scope of your business by helping you discover new markets relevant to your business.

Website Landing Page and Internet Marketing

The layout of your website plays an important role in increasing the ROI of your Internet marketing campaign. Audio-visual enhancements play a key part in increasing the efficiency of Internet marketing. Websites that add landing pages using videos experience an 86 percent increase in conversions. Articles with images get 94 percent more views than those articles without images.

Internet Marketing Techniques

Internet marketing has a broader reach than any other marketing technique, with more than two billion people using the Internet worldwide every day. This makes it important for businesses to implement an Internet marketing strategy for their company. Some of the most common techniques used to bring web visitors to a site through Internet marketing are:

- **Search Engine Optimization:** Search engine optimization, commonly referred  to as SEO, is a set of techniques that are used to optimize your website for major search engines, such as Google, Yahoo, and Bing. A well-optimized website is likely to have high ranks on Search Engine Result Pages (SERPS) for relevant keywords related to the business. For example: "SEO company in Dallas" is a keyword for a marketing company.
- **Pay Per Click:** Pay Per Click, or PPC, is a form of sponsored online advertising in which the advertiser pays only if a user clicks on their ad. This form of advertising is used in the sponsored links of search engines, as well as a wide range of other websites.
- **Social Network/Media Promotions:** Social media and social networking sites such as Facebook, Twitter, LinkedIn, Pinterest, and Instagram play an important

role in Internet marketing strategy due to their wide global reach. Advertisers can use these networks in a variety of ways to reach out to new customers and build relationships with existing ones.

In the pages ahead, we will take a detailed look at each of these Internet marketing strategies, to provide an overview of how Internet marketing can be implemented by small- and medium-sized businesses.

Internet Marketing Case Studies

Tesco, a British multinational grocery and general merchandise retailer headquartered in Hertfordshire, is one of the best examples of how Internet marketing has worked to revolutionize a brand. Tesco has become an online leader of six out of eleven markets of which it is a part. Tesco slates multichannel customers to be 2.2 times more important than solely in-store consumers.

Another case study carried out by Kenshoo on a leading retailer with more than 2,500 stores across the US, found that Paid Search+ Facebook Advertising strategies were significantly more effective than Search PPC strategies. In the study, customers who were exposed to Facebook + Paid Ads on search engines showed a 24 percent higher average order value than those exposed to a search engine ads strategy.

Five international brands that have reported a boost in customer satisfaction and lead generation following a content marketing strategy are Virgin Mobile, American Express, Marriott, Vanguard, and L'Oreal.

Besides the above-mentioned businesses, there are numerous online businesses that thrive purely on Internet marketing. Online portals such as Groupon, TicketMaster, Amazon, Yelp, Shopping.com, 1800flowers.com, PayPal, EBay, GoDaddy. com, etc. are typical examples of businesses that have been successful through online marketing strategies.

SEARCH ENGINES

Google

Yahoo!

Bing

comScore Explicit Core Search Share Report* July 2013 vs. June 2013 Total U.S. – Home & Work Locations Source: comScore qSearch			
Core Search Entity	Explicit Core Search Share (%)		
	Jun-13	Jul-13	Point Change
Total Explicit Core Search	*100.0%*	*100.0%*	*N/A*
Google Sites	66.7%	67.0%	0.3
Microsoft Sites	17.9%	17.9%	0.0
Yahoo! Sites	11.4%	11.3%	-0.1
Ask Network	2.7%	2.7%	-0.1
AOL, Inc.	1.3%	1.2%	-0.1

"Explicit Core Search" excludes contextually driven searches that do not reflect specific user intent to interact with the search results.

source: comscore

Percent of Share Search for Various Search Engines (June/ July 2013)

GOOGLE SEARCH ENGINE

Google is the world's most popular web search engine, handling over 3 billion searches a day, amounting to more than 100 billion searches each month (http://www.bbc.co.uk/news/technology-23866614). Originally developed in 1997, Google has come a long way from being a tool to search for words in a document to actually understanding what the users want and giving them what they need. This powerful search engine has added value to the web, making it possible to find the information you need within seconds.

With Google being the most popular search engine, search engine optimization has gone on to become synonymous with *Google optimization*, as webmasters work toward influencing their website rankings on Google. This is done through a complex process which patterns in Google's listings are discerned to determine *on-page* as well as *off-page* factors to improve rankings.

Google offers a variety of services to its members. Some directly relate to search engines, and others do not. The specialized searches allow you to find images, maps, news articles, products or services, blog entries, videos, scholarly papers, and much more. Non-search-related services offered by Google include Gmail, Google Docs, Google Maps, Google Earth, Google Translate, Google Plus, and YouTube.

- **Gmail** is Google's web-based e-mail program that anyone can sign up for, and it's free.
- **Google Docs** is a popular storage database that provides free storage space of up to fifteen gigabytes, with another one hundred gigabytes available for a cost of up to $4.99 per month. You can store documents, spreadsheets, presentations, and more with a Google Docs account.
- **Google Maps** allows users to view an address location or get driving directions.
- **Google Earth** uses Google Maps to create an interactive digital globe.
- **Google Translate** is a multilingual translation service that allows users to translate written text from one language to another.
- **Google+** is a social networking service by Google, with 540 million monthly active users; it is the second-largest social networking site in the world, trailing only Facebook (http://marketingland.com/google-hits-300-million-active-monthly-in-stream-users-540-million-across-google-63354).
- Google owns the popular video-sharing website **YouTube**, which is used to upload, view, and share videos.

Google also offers various additional services, including *Google Checkout, Google AdWords,* and *Google AdSense.* Google Checkout is designed to partner with merchants to make online purchases easier for customers. To create an account, users need to provide a credit or debit card number, which is stored in a secure database. This enables users to make future purchases without having to enter a card number each time.

AdWords allows companies to submit advertisements to Google that contain certain keywords related to their business. These tools serve as a way for Google to provide targeted advertising to users.

RECENT GOOGLE UPDATES

Google Penguin Update

The Google Penguin update, launched in April 2012, aims to flag websites that violate the Webmaster's Guidelines outlined by Google. This update was introduced by Google in an attempt to discourage black-hat SEO techniques, such as link schemes, which are used to manipulate inbound or outbound links to a website.

By making this update, Google has been able to identify thousands of websites that were spamming its search results. This was seen by many as a death knell for SEO and has forced webmasters to look for new, more authentic ways to improve their website rankings on Google. The message from Google was, as usual, to focus on creating high-quality content and employ white-hat SEO methods. Websites that are engaged in black-hat SEO techniques, such as buying links or getting them on link farms in order to achieve high ranks on Google, have been penalized by Penguin update.

How It Works

Google's Penguin update relies on human quality raters to determine the quality of a website. With hundreds of workers dedicated to ranking websites based on a set of predetermined factors, Google is given insight into possible changes.

However, this is just a part of the engineering testing process. Once a proposed change makes it through the initial test phases, it is subjected to a side-by-side test, which is a kind of blind taste test where, for a particular query, two sets of search results are assigned to human raters who give a comparative analysis.

Google Penguin primarily targets websites engaged in deliberate manipulation of search engine results using methods such as cloaking, creating mirror websites, generating fake links using software, etc. The feedback form, prepared by Google two days after this update was launched, involved users in the process by allowing them to report web spam that was still undetected and ask for a reconsideration if they felt their site was unfairly hit.

Effect on Search Listings

When the Penguin update was first launched in 2012, it impacted 3.1 percent of the total search queries on Google. The subsequent data refreshes impacted 0.1 percent and 0.3

percent of the total queries, respectively. This was followed by Penguin 2.0, which, with an impact of 2.3 percent, was the biggest tweak to the Penguin updates since the original update.

Sites that have been impacted by the Penguin updates can work toward getting the penalty lifted by cleaning up their back-link profile. However, merely focusing on the quality of links for your website is not enough, as it is equally important to work toward creating a positive user experience. The idea is to create and promote high-quality content, which provides value to its readers. The creation of natural back links to your website should come as a by-product of your efforts.

Google Panda Update

Introduced in February 2011, Google's Panda update aimed to curb sites with poor quality content and give way to those with high-quality content in Google's search results. The websites that were most affected by this update were those with a large amount of advertising. Those that experienced a positive impact in rankings following the update were news and social networking sites (http://www.wired.com/business/2011/03/the-panda-that-hates-farms). The update, which affected almost 12 percent of all search results on Google, helped to salvage the search engine's reputation at a time when Google's search quality was believed to be flagged.

How It Works

This update presents a development in the use of artificial intelligence, enabling its use in a more scalable manner. To begin, human quality testers were employed to rate thousands of websites based on their quality, trustworthiness, design, speed, and usability.

The next step was to use the new Panda machine-learning algorithm to identify the similarities between websites that received higher ranks, as well as those that were identified as low-quality websites. This helped to calculate the reputation of websites.

Since its introduction, the update has been modified various times to include new ranking factors and exclude previous ones, such as PageRank. The latest update has been the deployment of an over-optimization penalty, which aims to discourage sites that have inferior content but do a good job at SEO.

Difference Between Google Panda and Google Penguin Updates

While the Google Penguin update aimed to identify and penalize websites that are engaged in manipulating search engine results by following methods like cloaking, creation of doorway pages, and keyword stuffing in content, the Google Panda update was about reshuffling search engine ranks to make sure low-quality websites are not ranking on top of search engine results. Google Panda update affected websites having old, outdated, or less content. Also, websites that do not use images, videos, or info-graphics went down in search engine ranks.

Effect on Search Listings

The Google Panda update has had a significant impact on search listings and the web as a whole. Since it has had an impact on the rankings of an entire site, as opposed to just a certain section on the website, it has forced companies to change their entire business models and, in some cases, even shut down completely.

Once a website's rankings are affected by the Google Panda update, the most effective way to recover is to introduce pages with high-quality content to the site. However, Matt Cutts, head of Webspam at Google, emphasizes that simply rewriting content that was spammed due to lack of originality is not enough. The idea is to bring something new to the table. General, nonspecific content cannot be expected to rank well, even if it is not duplicated.

Once you make the necessary changes to your website, you might need to keep delivering positive results for a while before you can expect the Panda penalty to be lifted.

Google Hummingbird Update

Launched on Google's fifteenth anniversary, Google's Hummingbird update marks a significant step toward enabling a stronger interaction between Google and its users, providing more direct answers to search queries. Slated as the "future of search," this update allows users to be less mechanical and more natural when using the Google search engine. This is made possible by Google developing a better understanding of complex human language, as opposed to being limited to simplified keywords. The primary goal of this update is to weed out irrelevant resources from SERPs and identify the actual intent underlying searches.

How It Works

The Google Hummingbird is based on semantic search, which means that it lays focus on user intent, rather than being limited to individual search terms. This makes it possible for searches to be delivered based on the meaning of the whole sentence, instead of just a few keywords. For example, prior to the Hummingbird update, a query like "paying bills through Bank of America" would give you the home page of Bank of America's website as the top result. Post-Hummingbird update, for the same query, you would get a listing of the bill-payment section of Bank of America's website. Google achieves this outstanding question-answering ability through the combination of form-based queries and natural language techniques.

With this update, Google has added comparisons and filters to its algorithm, which make it possible to pull up the most attractive, engaging, and relevant response to the user's search. The basis of this update is that Google needs to understand queries, taking into account the grammatical structure and refined intent. Google is achieving this by adding three levels to search queries: complexity, comparison, and prediction. The result is a smarter search engine that understands concepts, rather than just words.

Effect on Search Listings

Google's Hummingbird update has not had any drastic impact on search listings, although it affected 90 percent of search queries. The guidelines of Google for webmasters who wish to safeguard themselves from any possible impact of this update are to focus on the quality and originality of content, and work toward having high-quality websites linking naturally to their website.

In fact, this update gives you a chance to separate yourself from your competition and be a part of Google's efforts to ensure that the websites that come up in searches are what its users want. The good news is that unlike some of Google's previous updates, Google's Hummingbird update has not been accompanied by any dramatic outcry about lost rankings by publishers. The effect of this update can be better defined as a query-by-query one, as opposed to one causing major traffic shifts.

YAHOO SEARCH ENGINE

Yahoo is a web search engine and portal that was launched in 1995. Yahoo Search is the world's third largest search engine, handling more than 2.15 billion searches every month. (http://www.comscore.com/Insights/Press_Releases/2013/11/comScore_Releases_October_2013_US_Search_Engine_Rankings). Yahoo bought its own search technology, Inktomi, in 2002, and went on to become an independent web-crawler based search engine in 2003. Since then, Yahoo has seen major ups and downs in its market share. In 2009, Yahoo entered into a deal with Microsoft, whereby its search engine is powered by Microsoft's Bing search engine.

Various Online Services Provided By Yahoo

Yahoo's search interface is now available in over thirty-eight international markets, and in at least forty different languages. One of the biggest success stories has been *Yahoo Answers*, where one can ask a question and get answers from the Yahoo community.

Yahoo News has also been widely successful, becoming the top global news site. (http://searchengineland.com/yahoo-top-news-site-google-second-people-spending-more-time-with-fewer-sites-32451).

Another highly popular service by Yahoo is its photo-sharing and video-hosting site, *Flickr*, which has more than 3.5 million new images uploaded on it daily. (http://www.theverge.com/2013/3/20/4121574/flickr-chief-markus-spiering-talks-photos-and-marissa-mayer).

Yahoo introduced a free e-mail service, *Yahoo Mail*, in 1997, which has more than 281 million active users (http://gigaom.com/2012/10/31/gmail-finally-beats-hotmail-according-to-third-party-data-chart/).

Yahoo Sports, launched in 1997, is now one of the world's most popular sports websites, delivering up-to-date news, scores, and information, with its fantasy sports leagues ranking among the most popular web services. According to a survey by ScoreWorldMetrix, Yahoo Sports is the number one online game site, with fans spending more time on it than on any other sports site (http://m.sportsbusinessdaily.com/Daily/Issues/2013/04/01/Media/Comscores.aspx).

Yahoo Finance provides accurate financial information, as well as updated information on various companies. With more than 37.5 million unique visitors every month, Yahoo Finance ranks as the top financial news and research website in the United

States (http://www.nytimes.com/2012/06/13/business/media/ cnbc-and-yahoo-finance-expand-partnership-to-online-video. html?_r=0).

The Internet advertising service provided by Yahoo is a keyword-based pay-per-click service named *Yahoo! Search Marketing*, which also provides PPC services through *Bing Ads*, with options like geotargeting, ad testing, campaign budgeting, and campaign scheduling.

BING SEARCH ENGINE

Previously known by names like MSN Search, Windows Live Search, and Live Search, Bing has been Microsoft's search engine offering, which was launched as Bing in 2009. Bing secured an 18 percent worldwide search share in Oct 2013, outdoing Yahoo, which received 11.3 percent (http://www.comscore.com/Insights/Press_Releases/2013/11/comScore_Releases_October_2013_US_Search_Engine_Rankings).

Bing's interface features, such as the daily changing of its background image, have made it highly popular across the web. It is also powered by attractive media features, such as the video thumbnail preview, image search, advanced filters, and video search.

Bing's instant answers range from sports and finance, to flight tracking, health information, mathematic calculations, advanced computations, and package tracking. Bing provides its users integration with various other web-based services, such as Hotmail, Facebook, Apple, and Windows 8. Bing Health provides access to relevant health information, with article results from experts.

Users can access detailed information on music, movies, television shows, and video games using *Bing Entertainment.* *Bing Maps* enables users to search for locations using a roadmap style view, a satellite view, or a hybrid of the two. Other services provided by Bing include *Bing Shopping, Bing Translator, Bing Travel,* and *Bing Videos.*

Bing offers a popular marketing service known as *Bing Ads,* which provides pay-per- click advertising on both Yahoo and Bing. The frequency of how often an advertisement is displayed using this service is determined by a combination of how much the advertiser is willing to pay and the click-through rate (CTR) of the advertisement. The success of advertising through this service widely depends on how effectively the ads are written and the relevancy of the advertisements to the searches made on the website.

Bing Ads allows advertisers to target a certain user demographic and advertise on specific days of the week or specific times of the day. It also provides Bing Ads editor, which allows advertisers to manage their campaigns offline. Another popular promotional service is *Bing Rewards,* which provides credit to users through special promotions and searches. These credits can then be redeemed for products like sweepstakes and gift cards. This program works on all desktop browsers, making it accessible to the entire web audience.

SEARCH ENGINE OPTIMIZATION (SEO)

SEARCH ENGINE OPTIMIZATION

Search Engine Optimization, commonly abbreviated as SEO, refers to the process of generating traffic to one's website through the organic search listings on major search engines like Google, Yahoo, and Bing. The ranking of a website is determined by what these search engines consider most relevant to the users. With hundreds of millions of search queries run on search engines every day, an effective SEO campaign can help business owners gain significant visibility among potential consumers.

The impact of search engine optimization is evident from a study by Outbrain that showed that search is the leading source of external traffic for all websites, driving a significant 41 percent of all traffic (http://searchengineland.com/search-sends-more-better-traffic-to-content-sites-than-social-media-study-says-72988). When you consider that over 2 billion people across the globe have access to the Internet, SEO can help to put your business out in front of about 40 percent of the world's population.

The origin of SEO dates back to the 1990s, where SEO simply referred to submitting the address or URL of a page, after which the search engine "spiders" would crawl over it, extract links, and index it. The phrase "search engine optimization" came into use in 1997, as webmasters began to realize the value of having high search engine ranks for their sites, giving way to both *white hat* and *black hat* strategies. SEO strategies where high search engine ranks are targeted by working on enhancing the quality of websites through useful content addition, descriptive tags, relevant images, descriptions, etc, are called white hat SEO techniques. Black hat SEO Techniques are techniques employed to trick search engines to rank websites high for certain keywords. Stuffing too many keywords in content, making multiple mirror websites, and using link-building software to get link backs are examples of black hat SEO techniques.

Since webmasters had more control to optimize their websites, search engines were bombarded with problems like link spamming and ranking manipulation. By 2007, the leading search engines had developed a set of undisclosed algorithms to reduce the impact of manipulation through black hat SEO techniques.

Other recent developments by Google to tackle ranking manipulation have been Google Panda update (2011), Google Penguin update (2012), and Google Hummingbird update (2013). These have worked toward allowing fresh content to rank quickly within search results, discouraging duplicate content, discouraging manipulative techniques, and improving Google's semantic understanding, respectively.

Present-day SEO is shifting focus to aspects like mobile SEO and geographically targeted SEO. After all, out of the 30 billion mobile searches carried out each year, 12 billion are targeted to find products or services in a particular city or locality. It is predicted that mobile searches will soon account for 50 percent of the total local searches (http://searchengineland.com/analyst-mobile-to-overtake-pc-for-local-search-by-2015-119148). The numbers are proof that SEO is one of the fastest evolving marketing techniques, and keeping up with its changing demands is essential to maintain your brand and staying competitive.

Need for SEO

Millions of people go online every day, searching for everything from the right "places to visit in Seattle" to "Chinese restaurants in Sydney." When the search engine results turn up, it is only the websites that make it to the first page of search engines that matter. A study by iProspect shows that 62 percent of the people searching online do not click past the first page.

SEO is a collection of techniques and strategies that can help your business secure the top positions on search engines for keywords relevant to their business. For instance, if you own a law firm in Texas, your business will benefit from being at the top of Google's first page when someone searches for "law firm in Texas" or say, "Texas divorce lawyer."

Here is a look at the top benefits of SEO for businesses:

- SEO helps the right people to find your website and is your first point of contact with your audience on the web. Studies show that 92 percent of the people who find your website get there from a search engine. This targeted audience has a high potential of converting into profitable leads for your business.
- SEO builds trust and credibility for your brand. When people carry out an online search, they psychologically tend to believe that top-ranking websites are trustworthy. In fact, Google is now referred to as a "reputation management machine."
- The high returns on investment generated through SEO make it one of the most affordable marketing strategies for your business.
- An active SEO program works as a 24/7 global sales force for your business.

- The results of SEO are long-term and sustainable, further adding to its value.

Here are some *sample small business SEO scenarios* to help you better understand the benefits of SEO:

Let's say you own Tim's Chinese Food in Austin, Texas. Having your website optimized for the search term "Chinese restaurant in Austin" can put you ahead of over 3,500 potential customers every month.

Consider another situation in which you own an Italian restaurant in Phoenix, Arizona. If you rank at the number one spot on Google for the keywords "Italian restaurant in Phoenix," you could get up to 4,000 clicks on your website through Google alone each month. Even if only 5 percent (i.e. 200) of these clicks convert into reservations, this could mean up to $10,000 in profit each month.

SEO will always remain a steadfast need for those who wish to remain ahead in the game through the undeniable benefits of increased traffic and visibility. The key is to work toward gaining knowledge and experience to keep meeting the changing demands of SEO.

SEO is broadly classified in two categories: on–page and off–page.

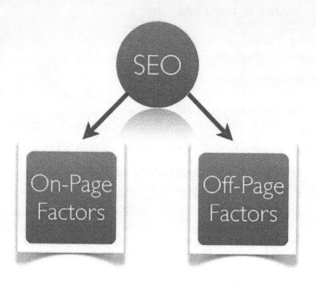

On-Page SEO

As the name suggests, On-Page SEO refers to a set of techniques surrounding the on–page factors of a web page that influence its search engine ranking. It basically consists of optimizing various elements of a web page. On-Page SEO is an integral part of the two-pronged approach to an effective SEO strategy, which involves a balance of on–page and off–page techniques. The origin of on–page SEO dates back to the beginning of search engines, when it was a simple technique used to compare websites.

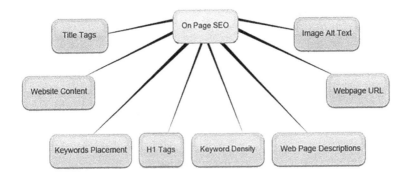

The major on-page factors include:

- Title tags of webpages
- Content of the website
- Keywords placement
- H1 tags
- Keywords density
- Webpage descriptions
- URL of webpages
- Webpage descriptions
- Image alt text

A perfectly optimized website from the on-page SEO perspective is one having unique content that provides in-depth information on a specific topic and has an SEO-friendly layout, in which the topic of the content is stated in the title tag, URL, page content, and in each image alt text on the page.

As a part of on-page SEO strategy, it is also important to have social network signs, videos, and info graphics on various pages of the website. The aim of on-page SEO is to tell search engines and human visitors what your website offers.

On-page SEO plays an important role in determining how your website ranks on search engines. Effective optimization techniques can help to ensure that your page ranks easily for targeted key terms. The technique involved in on-page SEO is very simple, and when done correctly, can help to significantly boost your ranking on major search engines.

Spammy SEO tactics like duplicate content, URL variants, hidden text, hidden links, keyword stuffing, and mirror pages should be avoided, as these can jeopardize your on-page SEO strategy. It is important to rely on ethical techniques, such as emphasizing search phrases through relevant content and working on generating inbound links naturally. The key is to stick to your niche while generating content for your website.

On-page SEO can be viewed as a mirror of your web page for search engines, which helps to increase the prominence of your website. Effective on-page SEO techniques have long-term and sustainable effects, and can help to decrease the need for extensive off-page optimization. Even though on-page SEO might not be as glamorous as off-page techniques, it plays an undeniable role in attaining high search rankings for your website.

Off-Page SEO: Introduction

Off-page SEO refers to a set of ongoing techniques that are performed on various portals and websites other than your website, with an aim to build links back to it. The better the number and quality of links you get, the higher you can expect to rank on search engines. The phrases *off-page SEO* and *link popularity building* are often used interchangeably. The links that you manage to generate to your website, by way of off-page SEO techniques, can be viewed as voters to nominate your website for the number one spot on search engines. However, off-page SEO is not limited to link-building and also includes other promotional techniques, beyond website design, which can be used to improve the position of a website in SERPs (search engine result pages).

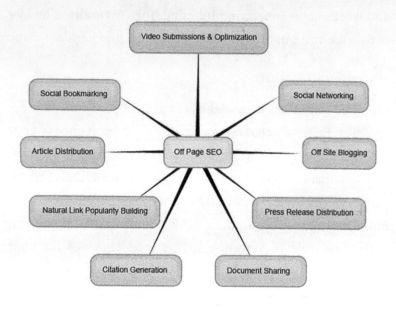

Various Off-Page SEO Techniques:

- Video submissions and optimization
- Social bookmarking
- Article distribution
- Natural link popularity building
- Citation generation
- Document sharing
- Press release distribution
- Off-site blogging
- Social networking

The mechanism of off-page SEO involves an elaborate process in which the search engine spiders *crawl* over the entire web, looking for links pointing back to your website. These links are then indexed, after which the algorithm determines the position that your website secures in the search results. It is important for these links to be natural and to have been generated by people who really loved the content on your website. Search engines favor links that come from websites that are recognized as authority figures in a particular niche.

Black hat SEO techniques were widely used to generate thousands of back links to websites in the past. They are now being viewed as web suicide, which can even cause your website to be deindexed by search engines. Link farms, which refer to websites that contain more than one hundred back links per page, are best to stay away from. The key should be to try to secure those hard-to-get links for your website, because the more difficult a link is to get, the more valuable it is likely to be.

Social media plays a key role in off-page SEO techniques, as search engines like Google use these social signals as a key metric to determine how useful a website is to users. The most important aspect of off-page SEO is great content.

Once you manage to create high-quality, original, useful, and relevant content for your website, everything else will take care of itself. Such content is self-promoting and will naturally get shared, automatically securing top ranks in search results. This, in combination with some effective link-building techniques and a robust social media strategy, is what it takes to top the game when it comes to off-page SEO.

Local SEO: Introduction

Carrying out an online search for, say, "Furniture Store in Houston, TX," yields business listings among the top results on Google. These listings correspond to the locations on the map at the top right corner of the result page. This is a clear depiction of what local SEO is all about. Local SEO basically works to create local relevance for your business, which is what search engines strive for when presenting results. The underlying idea is that it is better to be on first page of SERPs for a local keyword than on the second page for a more popular but generic search term. The importance of local SEO for businesses that primarily target a single geographical location cannot be emphasized enough.

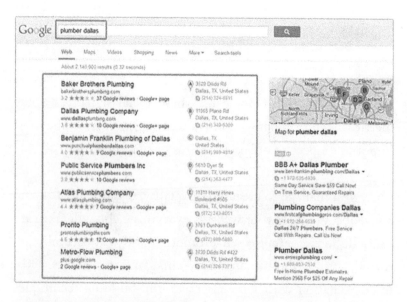

Your primary goal should be to show up in local listings. This can easily be achieved by signing up for a Google Places page for your business. Google Places is the new Yellow Pages that people are increasingly turning to when looking for a local business. In fact, you do not even need to own a website to engage in local SEO for your business. Having an optimized Google Plus page is enough.

When performing local SEO, it is extremely important to ensure that the business information you provide—including the address, phone number, and hours—is accurate. Having a fully filled-out profile with pictures can give your business a significant competitive edge.

The process of local SEO further involves securing listings from other sites, such as Bing, Yelp, Yahoo Local, Foursquare, etc, and then working to move up in the local listings using reviews, blogging, and multimedia updates. Local SEO plays a key role in marketing local businesses, and works best when used in conjunction with other techniques, such as organic SEO, social media, and brand awareness campaigns.

Generating quality business reviews is one of the most important ranking factors in local SEO, and helps search engines know that people love you. Add to that factors like social media signals, inbound links from local websites, and highly specific localized content, and you have a well-rounded local SEO strategy that can help you to dominate search engines for your local market. The focus in local SEO should always remain on quality, as opposed to quantity.

Local SEO is relatively simple and attainable, but requires a great deal of dedication, focus, and time. Businesses can definitely reap long-term rewards from local SEO, as search engines begin to recognize them as high-quality websites that offer a valuable user experience.

Local SEO Benefits

Local SEO has a wide range of benefits for small-scale businesses that mainly target a particular geographic location. The focus of this SEO strategy is on consumers who are looking for a specific service or product. Gaining visibility among this targeted audience can help to gain locally focused customers for your business and significantly boost your ROI.

Here is a look at some of the major benefits that local SEO offers to businesses:

- Local SEO leads potential customers to the landing page of your business, which contains relevant information related to your business, such as the address or phone number. This results in a much higher rate of conversion than if they were to be directed to the main page of your website.
- Local SEO gives you a greater chance of receiving high rankings for your business, owing to the lower competition faced by local keywords. It is more beneficial to rank on the first page for a local keyword

than to have a page-two rank for a generic but more popular keyword.

- Local SEO offers a cost-effective marketing strategy in comparison to PPC advertising campaigns. Effective local SEO strategies help you to target a smaller, but more compelling audience, which is more likely to use the product or service being offered by your business.

- Local SEO also helps you to build relationships with your customers, as it gives you an opportunity to use social media to your advantage and post information relevant to your local community. This helps to build an image of loyalty and trust among your local audience, increasing the chance of them shopping with you.

- Generating genuine reviews from your customers is a key aspect of local SEO, which can help in building a positive reputation for your business. People are a lot more likely to trust reviews from other customers than information that you have listed on your website.

- Local SEO goes hand-in-hand with mobile SEO, which means that a strong local SEO strategy for your business can also help to boost your online visibility when people search for your business using their mobile devices.

- You do not necessarily need to have a website to work on local SEO for your business. Having a well-optimized Google Places profile is enough to get started. This makes local SEO a highly practical option for small businesses with limited resources.

Measuring Success of SEO Campaigns

The methods adopted to measure the success of an SEO campaign for your business vary depending on the nature of your business and the desired goals from the campaign. The major factors that are analyzed to determine how effective a campaign is performing are known as Key Performance Indicators (KPIs). They can help you to measure the performance of your campaign and to gain data on how to improve the results of your campaign.

In order to analyze these KPIs, you need to choose an analytics program. While there are several online tools and measurements available for the purpose, Google Analytics is a free service that you can use to measure the success of your SEO campaigns.

It is important to establish a baseline by recording the first measurements before applying any SEO strategies to your website. Following this, you should maintain a weekly, monthly, and yearly record of these KPIs, to identify any changes that are seasonal and keep track of your SEO progress. Once you begin your SEO campaign, it will take at least four to eight weeks for these changes to be indexed by search engines, and several more weeks for them to affect your site's traffic.

The major KPIs include rankings, traffic, conversions, and number of websites linking back to your website.

Rankings

Keyword rankings are the most obvious yardstick to measure the efficiency of an SEO campaign. Tracking keyword rankings can help to identify various keywords that are benefitting your business and the ones that require increased attention.

When analyzing keyword rankings, it is equally important to measure the quality and volume of traffic being generated from first-page rankings, since these are useless if they do not deliver the right kind of traffic.

Traffic

The two major aspects involved when analyzing traffic are the traffic volume and traffic quality. Traffic volume refers to the number of visits generated for your business from organic search traffic. This is influenced by your target audience, the size of which determines the traffic volume you can expect from a successful SEO campaign.

The traffic quality is measured using metrics such as pages per visit, bounce rate, and average visit duration. Falling short on any of these parameters could point toward either an issue with your website or a problem with the type of traffic being attracted by the keywords you are targeting.

Conversions

Conversions are a relatively subjective KPI, the nature of which is defined by your specific business goals. For instance, if you aim to increase leads for your business, tracking conversions could mean analyzing aspects such as contact requests, quote requests, phone calls, appointment requests, etc.

You also need to take into account the actions of visitors on your website, keeping in mind that not all visitors are willing to buy. These conversions can be measured on the basis of social shares, newsletter subscriptions, whitepaper downloads, and other actions that indicate the interest of a visitor in the services being offered.

Along with conversions, it is also advisable to measure microconversions, which can help to identify specific issues in certain landing pages or links, which could be preventing people from fully converting. Microconversions are measured by setting up specific goals in analytics. For example, tracking a user's visit to a product category page or tracking a user's visit to a product detail page can be set up as microconversions.

Linkbacks/Back Links

Linkbacks or back links refer to links that return to your website from sources like social networking sites, blogs, bookmarking sites, and other websites in your niche. Search engines use these as a parameter to gauge the usefulness of your website and hence to determine the rank you achieve on SERPs.

PAY-PER-CLICK

WHAT IS PPC MARKETING?

Google Adwords
Yahoo   Bing

PPC marketing is short for pay-per-click marketing, which refers to search engine and display network marketing, comprising paid advertising techniques in which the advertiser pays a stipulated fee each time their ad either gets clicked on or is viewed. This differs from search engine optimization (SEO), where advertisers work toward getting visits to their website organically.

The mechanism by which PPC works involves a simple process whereby advertisers bid for the placement

Conn's Says Yes - Top Brands and Low Price Guarantee
www.conns.com/ ▾
Several Payment Options. Apply Now!
Easy Rent to Own - Find a Store - En Español

Rent To Own with RAC® - RentACenter.com
www.rentacenter.com/ ▾
No Credit Check Needed? Furniture, Appliances, TVs, Laptops & More.

Buddy's Home Furnishings - buddyrents.com
www.buddyrents.com/ ▾ 1 (855) 403 0931
Premium Furniture Up To 6 Months As Good As Cash! No Credit Checks

of their ad in the sponsored links of search engines (or display network websites).

Each time a user clicks on the ad and visits the website, the advertiser is required to pay a certain fee, usually a nominal amount. When a PPC campaign works correctly, the fee that the advertiser is required to pay is trivial compared to the profit that can be generated from a click that converts into a sale.

The major factor that determines the success of a PPC campaign is the effective research and selection of keywords. When choosing a PPC keyword list, the major consideration should be the relevance of the keywords. This research should be exhaustive, encompassing not just frequently searched terms in your area, but also long-tail keywords.

For example, if you own a furniture store in Dallas, Texas, your keyword list should not only include terms like "furniture store," "cheap furniture," and "bedroom furniture," but should also include terms like "where to buy kids bed," "tips on buying recliners," "living room furniture on sale," etc.

Once you have selected the most suitable keywords for your campaign, the next step is to organize those keywords into well-structured campaigns and ad groups, and establish optimized PPC landing pages. The ads used in PPC campaigns should be relevant and compel users to take action. It is important to be well equipped with knowledge regarding PPC marketing before starting off your campaign because search engines charge less for PPC campaigns that lead to landing pages that are useful and relevant for users.

The three most important factors that determine the success of your PPC campaign are:

- Keyword relevance
- Landing page quality
- Ad quality

PPC Platforms

Even though the list of PPC management services available on the web are practically endless, the two most popular options in PPC advertising are Google AdWords and Bing Ads, previously known as the Microsoft adCenter. Google AdWords is without question the most popular PPC advertising system available. It serves as an affordable platform for businesses to create ads that are visible on Google's search engine and its display network, including other Google properties. Bing Ads is the second most popular medium for PPC marketing, which includes PPC ads on both Bing and Yahoo! and their display network.

Benefits of PPC Marketing

Well-managed PPC campaigns that lead to optimized and relevant landing pages can serve as a cost-effective marketing technique for businesses. PPC marketing differs from traditional advertising techniques. When someone clicks on an ad, it means that they have already expressed their interest in the particular product or service being offered. Here is a look at some of the major benefits that businesses can gain from PPC marketing:

- The process of launching a PPC campaign is speedy, as compared to SEO, which requires a certain period of time from the point of initiation before it can go into effect.

- PPC attracts qualified leads and targeted traffic to your website, which makes it a highly profitable form of marketing. This is because PPC ads are designed to target specific keywords and demographics, leading to a high increase in the quality of website traffic generated.

- PPC marketing also serves as a good method to assess the performance of certain keywords for your website, at a low cost. Depending on the result of this low-risk testing, you can decide whether or not to carry out a full-site optimization for these keywords.

- The accurate reporting of data from a PPC campaign makes it easy to carry out an extensive tracking of the campaign and determine your Return On Investment. Moreover, since such a campaign requires you to pay only when an ad is clicked, this makes it easy to track conversions and manage costs.

- PPC marketing is affordable and cost-effective when compared to other marketing techniques, since it involves proven keyword expansion and effective bid-management techniques. Moreover, the fee that you need to pay when someone clicks on your ad is trivial when compared to the profit you can gain from such a click. Furthermore, if your ads lead to relevant landing pages that visitors find useful, search engines charge you less per click.

- PPC gives you a great chance to market your brand across an audience of millions using search engines every day. This potential for global exposure at such a minimal cost makes PPC marketing a one-of-a-kind marketing technique.
- PPC marketing allows you to choose the audience that you want to reach through your campaign. Using such a campaign could help you to reach an audience halfway across the world or to limit your reach to a certain geographical location.

It is important to note that besides multiple benefits that PPC has to offer, for some niches, running a PPC campaign might not be profitable. This makes it important to keep a check on the costs associated with PPC campaigns. Running a PPC campaign for keywords that are already bid at a higher rate will not be useful. Also, if you are selling a low cost product or service, PPC might not be beneficial for you.

Search Engine PPC Marketing

Search engine PPC marketing is one of the most popular types of PPC marketing. This involves bidding for ad placement in the sponsored links of search engines such as Google, Yahoo, and Bing. Search engine PPC marketing allows business owners to dictate search results by paying for advertisements, which is in contrast to organic search, where the results are natural and cannot be commercially influenced.

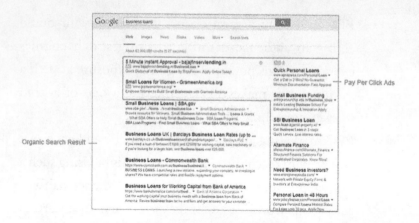

The stipulation underlying this form of PPC marketing is that advertisers need to make a payment only when someone clicks on the ad. This makes it highly beneficial as a marketing strategy for business owners, which explains why this form of paid search is a staple in Internet marketing.

A key aspect of search engine PPC marketing is using the right search terms for your business. These refer to key phrases that best describe the services or products offered by your business. The more relevant your offering is deemed to be by the search engines, the greater the efficiency of your PPC marketing campaign. Search engines run auctions for keywords based on their relevance to users. The two basic factors that influence these bids are the popularity of keywords and their profit potential.

The position of ads in search engine PPC marketing is decided by search engine algorithms, on the basis of the Click Through Rates (CTR) and bids made for the ads. Advertisers can make the most of these campaigns by starting the campaign slowly, taking time to analyze the effectiveness of keywords and advertisement. Even though ad campaigns can produce immediate results, the scaling up and tweaking of keyword lists can take up to three months. It is recommended to begin spending conservatively, and gradually progress based on how your ads perform.

Search analytics can help advertisers analyze profitable and emerging keywords for their target market on the basis market trends. This focus on metrics is a key aspect of search advertising campaign management, which can help to achieve the most profitable results for the least money.

The basic advantage offered by search engine PPC marketing is that it enables audience-based search optimization. Advertisers can use this form of Internet marketing to attract a targeted audience and offer them advertisements that cater to their immediate buying interests. This high relevance of search engine PPC ads, when used correctly, can lead to a significant boost to the ROI of businesses.

Display Advertisements

Display advertising is a form of online marketing in which businesses can display banner ads, also known as image or video ads, across a vast network of websites. The major focus of display advertising is to build a brand impression and spread online awareness about the services or products offered by your brand. This can be used cyclically with search engine-based PPC campaigns, with display ads creating a greater willingness among the target audience to respond to PPC ads.

A successful display advertising program is one that manages to strategically incorporate beautifully designed banners into the flow of the web page. The result has to be successful both visually as well as contextually. The idea is to create a display ad that manages to catch the user's attention without being distracting or annoying. However, the task does not end at designing the banner ad, but also extends to deciding the best possible placement for it.

Another critical aspect of display advertising is identifying your target audience and ensuring that the product or service being offered by your company logically fits their online interests. The success of such a program is gauged by the number of clicks and views that these ads get, as well as the sales and leads generated from them. If people are already searching for your brand or what you have to offer, then paid search should work for you. However, if you have yet to establish a brand image and build your online visibility, then display advertising is an excellent tool to spread the word across the web.

Display advertising gives you the liberty of controlling the extent of visibility that you would like to achieve. You can choose between a wide net or just a few select websites that you wish to target. The wide number of analytical tools helps you to track the performance of your display ad campaign and work toward a more granular optimization of your display ads. You can choose to get daily reporting of all the important numbers governing your ad campaign, including impressions, clicks, CTR, and conversions.

The best way to achieve success with display advertising is to analyze variables such as site quality and user interest, so as to identify what works best for your business. Display advertising gives you several options to choose from, including video ads, text, image, and rich media. The extent to which you can leverage this concept largely depends on the nature of your business and the audience you are targeting.

PAY PER CLICK PLATFORMS

Google
Adwords

Yahoo!   Bing
Network

GOOGLE ADWORDS

Google
Adwords

- Search advertising is one of the most effective and affordable forms of advertising available for online marketers. With 12 billion search queries a month, Google is undoubtedly the Mecca of search. Google's search marketing product, Google AdWords, helps you to reach the widest possible potential audience on Google and its ad partner websites.

- The process of initiating a campaign with Google AdWords is as simple as creating a Google AdWords account, constructing and naming your campaign, choosing some keywords to start with, setting a budget, waiting for approval, and following up to measure, modify, and repeat. AdWords does not charge you for creating ads, and you can create as many as you want.

- These ads are placed either on Google Search or on the Google Display Network. The ads on Google Search are limited to text, but cater to a highly specific audience that is already searching for your products, services, or brand. These ads will then be strategically placed on Google's sponsored section on its search results page. The ads on the Google Display Network, on the other hand, show up on other Internet websites and allow more flexibility in the types of ads, ranging from images to videos and rich text.

- You can launch multiple ads with different sets of keywords to start with, and then use Google's analytical tools to see which of these campaigns performed the best. Google requires you to set a specific budget that you are willing to spend on these ads. The duration of the ad campaign is based on this budget. This allows you to be in control of how much you spend on the AdWord campaign.

- The payment that you decide to pay each time an ad is clicked on is referred to as a *bid*. This bid is not decided for the campaign, but instead, for the particular keywords that constitute the campaign. The more valuable a keyword is for your business, the higher you should bid for it.

- This form of advertising is highly flexible and allows you to tweak your settings related to the keywords you choose, how much you pay, where they are placed, and for how long. These settings can be adjusted at any point. The intuitive tools offered by Google allow you to control several aspects of your campaign, including how it is displayed globally/ locally, the languages it is displayed in, and even where it should not appear.

BING/ YAHOO ADVERTISING-INTRODUCTION

Yahoo! Bing Network

- Bing Ads, formerly referred to as Microsoft AdCenter, is the pay-per-click advertisement platform offered by the Bing and Yahoo network. This is being viewed as a welcome alternative to Google AdWords, owing to the ads being displayed both on Yahoo and Bing. This reaches a potentially more diverse audience. This form of search advertising works on a simple concept whereby you create ads and bid on keywords. Having your ad at the top of the "sponsored links" section in the search results page grants significant visibility to your website amongst a highly targeted audience that is already searching for what you have to offer.

- The process of advertising on the AdCenter begins with creating an account on Bing Ads and providing some basic details for your campaign. You can then easily create and preview an ad and choose the keywords that you would like to advertise with. It is important to identify the right keywords and choose optimal keyword bids. Bing Ads allows you to create multiple ad groups under a single campaign. You can choose between displaying these ads only on the Bing-Yahoo search network, or on their syndicated partners search.

- The next step is bidding for your ads. You can choose to bid for search or content, or both. You also need to decide start and end dates for your campaign. The process of billing on the BingAds is relatively simple, since it allows you to pay using multiple payment methods. You only have to pay when someone clicks on your ad and visits your website. This makes this form of advertising highly affordable and cost-effective. The amount you pay for a single click is insignificant when compared to the potential profit you can earn from a successful lead.

- You can make use of the multiple tools in BingAds that allow you to analyze and optimize your ads. You can also generate reports that allow you to view the performance of your ads on the basis of parameters such as impression, clicks, amount spent, average CPC, CTR, and average position. The platform also offers a desktop tool that advertisers can use to manage their search campaigns from their desktop online or offline. Any changes that are made while offline can be synced with the user account once online.

Measuring the Success of a PPC Campaign

The success of a PPC campaign is directly measured by the goals achieved. A basic rule of thumb to measure campaign performance is to set up a monetary value for each goal targeted (whether it is generating a sale, a sign up, a page view, a download, etc.) and measuring that goal's value with the cost spent to achieve it. If the ROI for your campaign comes out to be positive, then you are moving in the right direction and you need to fine-tune your campaigns to increase your ROI. If it is negative, then you should rethink your PPC strategy and implement a new plan. If you are targeting competitive keywords, then you should keep a check on the money being spent, as they tend to be higher in cost per click.

As mentioned above, it is important to keep a check on what you spend and how much you spend, as most of the unsuccessful PPC campaigns are a result of overspending on wrong keywords with wrong budgets.

SOCIAL NETWORK/ MEDIA MARKETING

YouTube Facebook
Google + Pinterest
LinkedIn Twitter
Instagram

INTRODUCTION TO
SOCIAL NETWORKS

Social networking has gone on to become the buzzword of the online world, with websites like Facebook and LinkedIn redefining this sociological phrase. Social networking basically refers to the use of the Internet to connect with people in your network. Some of the most popular social networking and social media websites worldwide are Facebook, Google+, YouTube, Twitter, LinkedIn, Pinterest, Tumblr, Foursquare, Yelp, Instagram, and MySpace.

The basic purpose of these websites is to share ideas, pictures, posts, activities, and other items of interest among people who are a part of your network. In this way, social networking websites help to give a face to social interactions that would otherwise be invisible. They can also be used for other activities, such as organizing events, chatting, or playing games. The concept of networking comes from the connections that are formed with friends of friends or followers. Along with serving as a great means to connect with friends, social networks have also emerged as a trusted recommendation system.

With more than 73 percent of online adults in America being a part of a social network online, this trend is here to stay (http://pewInternet.org/Commentary/2012/March/Pew-Internet-Social-Networking-full-detail.aspx). The popularity of social networks can be attributed to the social value that they grant their users. This includes useful information, personal relationships, and the ability to form groups based on shared interests. Here is a look at some of the most prominent social networks and what they offer:

- **Facebook:** Facebook is the world's most popular social networking site, with over 1.11 billion members. Users on this site create personal profiles, following which they can add other users as "friends," share and view status updates, upload photos and videos, exchange messages, and keep in touch with people added to their profile.

- **Google+:** Google+ is a social networking site that is widely described as an "identity service." With more than 540 million active users, it is the world's second largest social networking site. It has a popular Hangout feature that allows users to carry out free video conferencing with up to ten people.

- **YouTube:** YouTube is a video-sharing website owned by Google, where users can upload, share, view, and comment on videos.

- **Twitter:** Twitter is a micro-blogging site that enables users to share tweets, which are text updates of less than 140 characters. It has more than 500 million users, and handles more than 1.6 billion search queries a day.

- **LinkedIn:** LinkedIn caters to people in professional occupations, allowing them to create an online professional identity and build a network with trusted contacts.

Facebook Marketing

Facebook is a valuable tool for businesses engaging in online marketing, as it helps you to reach out to existing and potential customers, and actively promote your business. You can use Facebook to build an online community for your business, with the potential of turning a part of that community into customers. This marketing tool is not just free (except paid advertising), but also immensely powerful, which explains why nearly every business has a Facebook business page.

A Facebook page helps to serve as an identity for your business, allowing you to share basic information, such as your business name, address, contact details, and a brief description of what you offer. It also works as an excellent tool to build your brand image and identify your business through product offerings, services, links, images, and posts on your customizable page. This serves as a platform to showcase your Unique Selling Propositions, the attractiveness of your products/services, and to establish brand loyalty for your business.

In addition to this, you can also use Facebook for classic marketing by having your ad appear in the side column of the Facebook site. These ads enable demographic targeting, fixed budgets, ad testing, and built-in performance analysis tools. Businesses also use several other marketing tactics on Facebook, including campaigns, contests, sweepstakes, and promotions.

You can further increase the reach and impressions of specific posts on your Facebook business page by paying a certain amount. These posts, which are referred to as *promoted posts*, have a greater chance of being seen in the newsfeeds of users.

Sponsored stories can also be used to promote your Facebook page. Sponsored stories can highlight interactions by people with your Facebook page on their friends newsfeeds. Sponsored stories are different than promoted posts, as they just show interactions between people and your page, while promoted posts shows what you share on your timeline.

E-commerce websites can benefit greatly from having a Facebook login option. Statistics show that four of every five users prefer to login through Facebook. Additionally, search engines love social media platforms, which mean that actively engaging on Facebook can also help to boost your website's ranking on SERPs.

The key to a successful Facebook marketing campaign is to be authentic, responsive, and consistent. It is a good idea to keep your audience engaged to provide frequent feedback, considering that Facebook surveys boost post popularity by a whopping 139 percent, exceeding the impact of any other type of post. When creating Facebook posts for your business page, remember not to get carried away with blatant self-promotion, and instead to focus on posts that resonate with users and actively engage them. After all, no one wants their timeline to be filled with a constant hard sell.

With nearly 50 percent of the world's Internet users active on Facebook, the marketing potential of this social networking site is unmatchable. A well-planned social media strategy on Facebook can help to increase targeted traffic to your website and significantly boost sales.

Twitter Marketing

Twitter is a social networking site where users can share 140-character long text messages, known as Tweets, which are available to other users across the world. Twitter can serve as a great marketing tool for your business, helping you to communicate directly with customers and business prospects, while also keeping up with the latest trends in your business niche. The two basic purposes solved by Twitter are customer service and content discovery.

It also comes with the benefits of social networking, which include sharing useful content, deals, and promotions with your followers. Building a Twitter account is enough to make you instantly more findable on search engines. The key elements for an optimized profile include a username, your business name, a profile image, a header image, your profile bio—preferably including your URL and location—and your background image.

Twitter gives you a chance to develop a brand image for your business, allowing you to demonstrate the values that you stand for. It is a good idea to keep your language completely basic while marketing on Twitter, instead of resorting to boring sales lines. If people find the information you are sharing on your Twitter account useful, this can serve as a mechanic to guide them to your website. The idea is to value the time of your followers, so that they offer you their attention when you need it.

When used correctly, Twitter is a highly effective and popular marketing tool for your business. It can help you to expand your network, guide visitors to your website/blog, generate leads for your business, build a professional online brand, and connect you to people who matter to your business. With a billion tweets being sent out every week on Twitter, the key to succeeding is to make the most of the immense exposure it offers, without becoming a part of the noise.

The impact of Twitter for marketing your brand can be understood by the following statistics:

- Average number of monthly active users on Twitter: 115 million
- Number of new Twitter users signing up every day: 135,000
- Number of days it takes for 1 billion tweets: 5
- Number of tweets that happen every second: 9,100

Not only does Twitter help people find out about what you offer, but it is also highly effective in converting these followers to profitable leads. Statistics show that 36 percent of marketers succeeded in finding a customer via Twitter.

LinkedIn Marketing

Having a LinkedIn profile is also a very important social media strategy for your business. With one person creating a LinkedIn account every second, the exposure granted to business owners by this social network is unmatchable. When used correctly, LinkedIn, which has emerged as the number one professional network, can help you to generate leads for your business and see an actual rise in your ROI.

Your LinkedIn profile works as an online resume showcasing your education, skills, experience, and any significant achievements. Joining groups in your niche on LinkedIn can work like magic, serving as a platform to share expert knowledge, engage in questions and answers, and even conduct industry surveys. The newsfeed works a lot like Twitter, helping you to build a trustworthy and consistent brand image.

The recent changes made by LinkedIn for professional profiles and company pages has further increased its worth for business owners, giving them better opportunities to market their expertise and increase traffic and leads. LinkedIn can help to boost traffic to your website, with the network being responsible for a whopping 64 percent of all visits from social media channels to corporate websites (http://econsultancy. com/blog/63616-linkedin-users-are-more-interested-in-your-company-stats).

LinkedIn is used by over 65 million business professionals, making it the world's largest audience of business professionals. Most of these professionals belong to the elite class, with 28 percent of LinkedIn users having an annual income of more than $104,000, and 50 percent of them being decision makers for their company. Add to that over 225 million registered users from over 200 countries on the network, and you have the ideal playground for business marketing.

You can choose between a passive or an active approach to promote your business on LinkedIn. Passive marketing on LinkedIn is as simple as creating a profile on the network, building connections, and keeping your account updated. This is enough to give your business the exposure it needs when people hunt for your products/services, get you valuable introductions, and display word-of-mouth testimonials in the form of recommendations.

Aggressive LinkedIn marketing, on the other hand, is a way to take maximum advantage of all that this network has to offer. This involves a much more consistent approach, in which you post regular status updates, actively participate in groups, send messages and invitations to relevant people in your network, make the most of LinkedIn advertising, and even consider a paid LinkedIn membership, which offers benefits like additional contact options and powerful sales features.

g+ Google Plus for Marketing

Google+ has enjoyed tremendous growth ever since its launch in 2011, going on to become the world's second most popular social network, with more than 359 million users (http://www.businessinsider.com/google-plus-is-outpacing-twitter-2013-5?IR=T). These statistics are enough to understand why Google+ marketing has gone on to become an indispensable tool for businesses engaging in online marketing. Although Google+ has not been around as long as its competitors, its unique features and SEO capabilities more than make up for the late start.

Interestingly, having one hundred active followers on your Google+ profile can boost your SERP rankings on Google by an astounding fourteen points! Google+ marketing is especially important for businesses that are heavily embedded in YouTube, since YouTube comments are fueled by Google+.

Here is a look at the top features that Google+ offers to online marketers:

- The incorporation of hashtags into Google+ has boosted its SEO performance significantly, with users now being able to perform searches on this social network directly.

- Another feature that makes Google+ stand out in the world of social media marketing is the Google+ Hangouts. This free app enables users to chat with up to ten people at a time, making it a valuable marketing tool. Interestingly, you can choose to make these conferences publicly viewable by broadcasting them on your YouTube channel.

- Google+ Circles ensures that your message reaches out to a relevant audience. You can further boost engagement by tailoring specific messages for specific circles.

- You can use the Google+ Stream feature to give instant updates to people in your circle. This is a great marketing technique for online businesses, as it can convey information regarding product launches or special offers to interested parties in real time.

- The "Plus One" button on Google+ works as a stamp of reliability for content related to your business and can be shared on individual web pages. Businesses can benefit greatly from this button, as it serves as an invaluable form of word-of-mouth publicity.

Google+ has quickly established itself as the social network for professionals, offering significant advantages over Twitter and Facebook. When marketing your business on Google+, you do not need to worry about limiting your posts or messages to 140 characters or being taken seriously on a network crowded with teens posting birthday pictures. In order to make the most of Google+ marketing for your business, it is important to create a powerful and complete profile, add relevant people to your circles, and develop a consistent content strategy.

Social Media Marketing

With the advent of popular social networks like Facebook, Twitter, Google+, LinkedIn, etc., social media marketing has gone on to become one of the most effective media for businesses to reach out to a relevant audience. Businesses all over the world are increasingly using social media sites to gain traffic and draw attention to their websites. The techniques that are used for this purpose comprise social media marketing, which encompasses sharing business information, building a network of relevant users, and posting regular content updates related to your business.

One of the greatest tools that social media marketing offers businesses is Electronic Word of Mouth (eWOM), which can help to significantly boost the online reputation of the products or services offered by a business. The increasing number of users accessing social networking sites through their mobile devices has further contributed to globalizing the impact of these websites in business promotions.

YouTube (YouTube.com) is among the most popular social media websites, which enables advertisers to create targeted video campaigns for different audiences. Ever since Google's purchase of YouTube, Google's search algorithm gives significant preference to websites with videos over those without. The great thing about creating a video for your website on YouTube is that you can simply embed the link on your website, saving bandwidth and enabling quicker loading time. From tutorials on how to operate products to funny videos, the marketing opportunities to explore with YouTube are endless.

Pinterest (Pinterest.com) has also gained popularity as a social media marketing channel, catering to the diversified social media use of Americans. From B2B models to B2C models, everyone can benefit from Pinterest. This photo-sharing social media network enables users to create image collections based on different themes, which can then be "repinned" by other users. You can make the most of this site by creating different boards to represent your business.

StumbleUpon (StumbleUpon.com) is another great site that can work wonders to boost traffic to your website. It can also help you to find sharable content online and learn what type of content works best. StumbleUpon can best be described as a merger between a content-discovery site, a search engine, and a bookmarking site. The key to making the most out of this website is to create content that is entertaining, informative, and relevant for your audience.

Social media promotions, when done correctly, can help to engage fans, build awareness for your products/services, and help to drive conversions to sales for your website.

Instagram (Instagram.com) is another popular service that can help you promote your business to the masses. It allows you to take pictures and videos and share them on various social networking platforms, such as Facebook, Twitter, Tumblr, Flickr, etc. You can modify your pictures before uploading them. Instagram also allows you to create your profile and share your pictures, videos, and other information for people to view. With 150 million active users (data for Sept 2013), having a profile on Instagram can give good exposure to your business.

MEASURING RESULTS

MEASURING INTERNET MARKETING PERFORMANCE WITH WEB ANALYTICS

Web analytics play a key role in determining how successful your Internet marketing campaign is by giving you a bird's eye view of how advertising is helping to boost the performance of your website for your business. "Web analytics" is essentially a complex term, encompassing tracking, measurement, and analysis of Internet data for a quantitative analysis of marketing initiatives.

With web analytics, you no longer need to wonder about which part of your marketing strategy is working and which is going to waste. It gives you a transparent and clear view of whether your investment is paying off, and also helps you to identify chokepoints that prevent conversion goals from being completed.

The first step to using web analytics for Internet marketing is determining the needs of your company. Analysis tools like Google Analytics can help to measure the abandonment rate between any two steps in your sales path. This can be instrumental in identifying areas that need improvement.

You then need to quantify your objectives based on the nature of your business website. These objectives could be increased sales, decreased marketing expenses, increased readership of content, segment lead generation, increased customer satisfaction, or decreased customer support inquiries, based on your individual business goals. A good analytics tool can then help you to measure these clearly defined objectives.

Next, you need to define metrics for your business, which is basically a definition of what to measure to boost your marketing results. These could include a measure of loyalty, churn rate, user behavior showing that the user is ready to buy, number of unique visitors to your site, time spent by visitors on your site, cross-selling and up-selling, profiling, etc.

With your needs, objectives, and metrics clearly identified, you can now move on to collecting data using either web server log data or page-tagging tools. Once your data is collected, the next step is recording it, which should start from a baseline, from which you can gradually track improvement for each objective.

Once you have data over a sufficient period, you need to identify and implement improvement strategies. This can be done by measuring different conversion rates, such as downloads, lead-generation forms, and search functions for improvement, as well as measuring online business activities like sales process, registration process, onsite search, etc.

You can implement the A/B testing tool to monitor the effect of proposed changes to your website. This method allows you to test different versions of your site against a benchmark and then quantify their performance to see which strategy works better.

Finally, it is important to accurately measure the ROI that your Internet marketing strategies are generating, as mentioned in the "Internet Marketing Campaign ROI" section, for a clear idea of your marketing accountability. When it comes to measuring results of an Internet marketing campaign, there is never a point where you can sit back and relax. This process has to be ongoing, where you continuously monitor your conversions and keep tweaking your goals and metrics to maintain a competitive edge.

INTERNET MARKETING CAMPAIGN ROI

Being able to calculate the Return on Investment (ROI) for your online marketing campaigns is important for understanding what's working and what's not, so as to be able to determine whether it is worth investing more money in your campaign. Without a means to measure the ROI from your online marketing campaigns, you could have the best advertisements at the most strategic positions on the Internet, but these are of no use unless you know how they are performing.

A simple *formula to calculate the ROI* for your Internet marketing campaign is:

(Gross Profit – Marketing Costs)

—————————————————— X 100

Marketing Costs

This formula will give you a percentage, which, ideally, should exceed 100 percent. For instance, if your ROI comes out to be

150 percent, that means that you are making $1.50 for every $1.00 spent on the campaign.

However, this calculation is not always so straightforward, since you also need to take into account the customers who see the campaign, even if they do not take immediately make a purchase, as well as lifetime customers gained through the campaign who make multiple purchases. Both these factors can be taken into account by assigning a value for each impression and an estimated lifetime value for the profit from each customer, respectively.

Another effective way of calculating the ROI from your marketing campaign is creating a marketing scorecard as shown below:

Date range:	01/27/14–01/28/14	Marketing Scorecard					
Campaign	Ad Spend	Visits	CPC	Conversions	Conversion Rate	Cost per sale
Total						

The campaigns in the scorecard should be broken down into different channels and sources. For instance, banner ads should be separated by site. Such a scorecard is a simple tool that can help to involve different members of the organization in analyzing the ROI from the campaign.

In addition to calculating the ROI for your campaign using the aforementioned methods, you can also perform online tracking using tools like Google Analytics to track responses for all of your campaigns and the source of traffic.

While it is critical to link Internet marketing to financial performance, it is important for investors to realize that marketing is not a one-time capital project. It makes more sense to view online marketing as an expense, as opposed to an investment, in order to be able to make the most of its contribution to business goals.

GLOSSARY

AdWords	Google's Internet marketing platform that allows users to place advertisement on Google search and various websites under Google's network.
Analytics	A program that tracks and records users behavior on a website. Google Analytics is a popular analytics program.
Back Link	Any incoming link to a website from another website.
Black Hat SEO	SEO tactics that are used to trick search engines in order to get high ranks on search results.
Cloaking	Process of delivering different content to search engine programs than that seen by human users. It is a common black hat technique.
CPC	Cost Per Click: the rate paid by an advertiser for a single click.

CPM	Cost Per Thousand Impressions: the cost paid by an advertiser to display an advertisement to thousands of users.
Doorway Pages	A web page created to attract traffic from search engines.
Info-graphics	Visual image (chart/diagram) used to present information or data.
Keyword	A phrase that a user enters in a search engine to find a product/service/information.
Keyword Density	Percentage occurrence of a particular keyword in a web page.
Keyword Stuffing	Adding an inappropriately high number of the same keywords on a web page to get high search engine ranks.
Landing Page	A web page on which a user lands when they click on search engine listings or advertisements.
Lead Generation	Process of generating an inquiry from a website.
Link Building	Process of getting inbound links to your website.
Link Farm	Group of websites linking with each other's.
Local SEO	Search engine optimization techniques used for getting high ranks for geographically targeted search queries.

Long Tail Keywords	A set of descriptive keywords. For example, "water dispenser suppliers in Dallas, TX."
Meta Tags	HTML header tags used to define a web page.
Mirror Websites	Websites that are an exact replica of already existing websites. Mirror websites are used to capture multiple SERPs.
Off-Page	Activities performed on online portals, websites, etc., other than the one that is to be ranked high on search engine listings.
On-Page	Activities performed on the website that is to be ranked high on search engine listings.
Organic Search Results	Search results for a particular query other than sponsored ads.
Page Rank	An algorithm user by Google to rank websites based on their importance.
ROI	Return On Investment
Search Engine	A program used to find products, services, or information from different websites on the World Wide Web.
Search Engine Optimization	SEO: a process to achieve high search engine ranks for particular keywords.
Search Listings	Results generated by search engines for a particular search query.
SEM	Search Engine Marketing: it includes SEO, online advertisements, paid listings, etc.

SEO	Search Engine Optimization: it is a process to achieve high search engine ranks for keywords.
SERP	Search Engine Ranking Page
Web Crawler	A program designed to automatically visit websites and analyze them for required parameters and store information about them for further processing.
Whitepaper Downloads	In whitepaper downloads, a whitepaper (document containing reliable information from authority sources) is provided to users for downloading through different document-sharing portals.

BIBLIOGRAPHY

Page 9

Biswas, Soutik. "Digital Indians: Ben Gomes." BBC News. Last modified June 16, 2014. http://www.bbc.co.uk/news/technology-23866614

Page 10

McGee, Matt. "Google Hits 300 Million Active Monthly "In-Stream" Users, 540 Million Across Google." Marketing Land. October 29, 2013. Accessed June 16, 2014. http://marketingland.com/google-hits-300-million-active-monthly-in-stream-users-540-million-across-google-63354.

Page 14

Levy, Steven. "TED 2011: The 'Panda' That Hates Farms: A Q&A With Google's Top Search Engineers | Business | WIRED." Wired.com. March 1, 11. Accessed July 2, 2014. http://www.wired.com/business/2011/03/the-panda-that-hates-farms.

Page 19

Lella, Adam. "ComScore Releases October 2013 U.S. Search Engine Rankings." ComScore, Inc. November 13, 2013. Accessed July 2, 2014. http://www.comscore.com/Insights/Press-Releases/2013/11/comScore-Releases-October-2013-US-Search-Engine-Rankings.

Page 20

Sterling, Greg. "Yahoo Top News Site, Google Second; People Spending More Time With Fewer Sites." Search Engine Land. December 24, 2009. Accessed July 2, 2014. http://searchengineland.com/yahoo-top-news-site-google-second-people-spending-more-time-with-fewer-sites-32451.

Page 20

Jeffries, Adrianne. "The Man behind Flickr on Making the Service 'awesome Again'" The Verge. March 20, 2013. Accessed July 2, 2014. http://www.theverge.com/2013/3/20/4121574/flickr-chief-markus-spiering-talks-photos-and-marissa-mayer.

Page 20

Molla, Rani. "Gmail Finally Beats Hotmail, According to Third-party Data [chart]." Gigaom. October 31, 2012. Accessed July 2, 2014. http://gigaom.com/2012/10/31/gmail-finally-beats-hotmail-according-to-third-party-data-chart/.

Page 20

Fisher, Eric. "Yahoo Sports Tops ComScore's First Media Metrix Multi-Platform Rankings." SportsBusiness Daily. April 1, 2013. Accessed July 2, 2014. http://m.sportsbusinessdaily.com/Daily/Issues/2013/04/01/Media/Comscores.aspx.

Page 21

Stelter, Brian. "To Bolster Web Reach, CNBC Joins With Yahoo." The New York Times. June 12, 2012. Accessed July 2, 2014. http://www.nytimes.com/2012/06/13/business/media/cnbc-and-yahoo-finance-expand-partnership-to-online-video.html?_r=0.

Page 22

Lella, Adam. "ComScore Releases October 2013 U.S. Search Engine Rankings." ComScore, Inc. November 13, 2013. Accessed July 2, 2014. http://www.comscore.com/Insights/Press-Releases/2013/11/comScore-Releases-October-2013-US-Search-Engine-Rankings.

Page 28

McGee, Matt. "Search Sends More & Better Traffic To Content Sites Than Social Media, Study Says." Search Engine Land. April 14, 2011. Accessed July 2, 2014. http://searchengineland.com/search-sends-more-better-traffic-to-content-sites-than-social-media-study-says-72988.

Page 29

Sterling, Greg. "Analyst: Mobile To Overtake PC For Local Search By 2015." Search Engine Land. April 20, 2012. Accessed July 2, 2014. http://searchengineland.com/analyst-mobile-to-overtake-pc-for-local-search-by-2015-119148.

Page 70

"Social Networking Fact Sheet." Pew Research Centers Internet American Life Project RSS. Accessed July 2, 2014. http://pewInternet.org/Commentary/2012/March/Pew-Internet-Social-Networking-full-detail.aspx.

Page 77

Fergusson, Marcus. "LinkedIn Users Are More Interested in Your Company: Stats." Econsultancy. October 18, 2013. Accessed July 2, 2014. http://econsultancy.com/blog/63616-linkedin-users-are-more-interested-in-your-company-stats.

Page 78

Watkins, Thomas. "Suddenly, Google Plus Is Outpacing Twitter To Become The World's Second Largest Social Network." Business Insider. May 1, 2013. Accessed July 2, 2014. http://www.businessinsider.com/google-plus-is-outpacing-twitter-2013-5?IR=T.

Page 82

"Instagram." Instagram. Accessed July 2, 2014. http://blog.instagram.com/post/60694542173/150-million.

ABOUT THE AUTHOR

A well-known and respected member of the information technology industry, Abdul B. Subhani is an internet marketer, entrepreneur, and public speaker. Abdul was born in Multan and raised in Islamabad, Pakistan. While in Pakistan, he was involved in many community service projects and was a Boy Scout as a young student. He came to the United States in 1998, earned his master's in Information Systems, and founded Centex Technologies, an IT consulting company with offices in Central Texas, Dallas, and Atlanta.

In 2002, he became an adjunct faculty member for Computer Science, Distance Learning Department & Continuing Education Department of Central Texas College. He has developed numerous non-credited computer courses for Central Texas College Continuing Education Department and written a book on Microsoft Outlook that was published by Central Texas College. He is also an adjunct faculty member of Texas A&M University, Central Texas, in the Computer Information Systems Department.

With experience working with technology gurus, business owners, and more, Subhani is able to speak at technology and marketing conferences around the country. He has been a frequent keynote speaker, moderator, and panelist at leading international technology conferences. He has also given speeches to thousands of students at colleges and universities.

Subhani has a bachelor's degree in Computer Technology and a master's in Information Systems. While working on his undergraduate and graduate degree, he subsequently earned advanced credentials as a Microsoft Certified Systems Engineer, Certified Ethical Hacker, Certified Fraud Examiner, Certified Internal Controls Auditor, Certified Internet Marketer, Certified Project Manager in E-Business, Certified E-Commerce Consultant and CompTIA Network+, Security+, and is certified in Risk and Information Systems Control.

He is actively involved in his community as a member of Exchange Club, chairman of the Boys & Girls Clubs of Central Texas, Vice Chairman of the chamber of commerce, a board member for Central Texas College Foundation, a board member of Independent School District Education Foundation, the chair of the Technology Committee at the Career Center of Killeen Independent School District, and a board member of Texas A&M University Central Texas Alumni Association.

www.ingramcontent.com/pod-product-compliance
Lightning Source LLC
LaVergne TN
LVHW042134040326

832903LV00001B/3